Creative Easter Crafts for Kids

Activity Book

warner press KiDs

warnerpress.org

305800212877

Table of Contents

How to Use This Book

Creative Easter Crafts for Kids has been designed for use at home or in a classroom setting with kids ages 8 and up. Depending on their skill and reading level, children may be able to create the crafts independently; however, we recommend that a parent or teacher be available to review the craft for suitability and offer assistance if needed. The crafts may be done in any order.

Each craft includes a Scripture passage to look up and read in the Bible, as well as a memory verse. A short devotional highlights a portion of the Easter story or other related theme. Questions help the child reflect on the story and apply it personally.

Detailed instructions and illustrations help make the craft easy enough for most children to understand. Many crafts are made with items you most likely already have at home or in the classroom. A few may require a trip to your local discount or craft store.

Our prayer is that the lessons in this book will help children grow in their faith and understanding of the Bible as they have fun exploring and developing their creativity.

Countdown to Easter Matthew 20:17–19

On the third day he will be raised to life!

MATTHEW 20:19 (NIV®)

The season of Lent begins on Ash Wednesday and ends on the Saturday before Easter. Ash Wednesday gets its name because people go to church and have their foreheads marked with ash to show they are sorry for their sins and want to return to God. Easter, not counted as a day of Lent, is the Sunday we celebrate Jesus rising from the dead.

Lent lasts 40 days, not counting Sundays. The 40 days remind us of the time Jesus spent fasting and being tempted in the wilderness by Satan. During the season of Lent, many people fast—or give up something—to help them remember the sacrifice Jesus made when He died for our sins on the cross.

During Lent, people usually give up one of their favorite foods or something else that they really enjoy—like watching TV or using social media, for example. As they remember not to eat that food or watch that show, people spend some time praying or reading the Bible, thinking about Jesus and His life, death, and resurrection.

At this special time of year, many churches decorate with the color purple. Purple symbolizes mourning as we remember Jesus' death and also royalty because Jesus is our King.

Questions:

1. What do you and your family do during the season of Lent?
2. Do you give up something for 40 days? If not, what could you give up that would help you think of Jesus?
3. Jesus was tempted, and so are we. What do you do when you are tempted to do something wrong?
4. What are some qualities that good kings have? How is Jesus like a king? How is He different?
5. We often count the days before an event that we look forward to. What do you like best about Easter?

This paper chain will help you count the days until Easter. When you remove a piece of the chain, take some time to pray or read your Bible and remember Jesus.

Materials:

- Pastel construction paper
- White construction paper
- Scissors
- Tape, glue, or stapler
- Markers or crayons

Directions:

1. Begin by cutting 1" x 9" strips of construction paper. You will need 40 strips of pastel colors and 7 strips of white.
2. Choose one pastel strip and write "Ash Wednesday" on it. Loop the paper so that the words show and fasten it to make a circle. Use pastel strips to form the next 3 links in the chain. Use a white strip for the next link, to represent Sunday, then pastel strips for the next 6 links. Repeat this pattern 4 times. On the next white strip, write "Palm Sunday." Attach link to the chain, making sure the words show. Add 3 pastel strips. On the fourth pastel strip, write "Maundy Thursday," and on the fifth pastel strip, write "Good Friday." Add one more pastel strip. On the final white strip, write "Easter."
3. Hang the strip with Easter at the top and Ash Wednesday at the bottom.
4. Remove a link each day to count down the days of Lent.

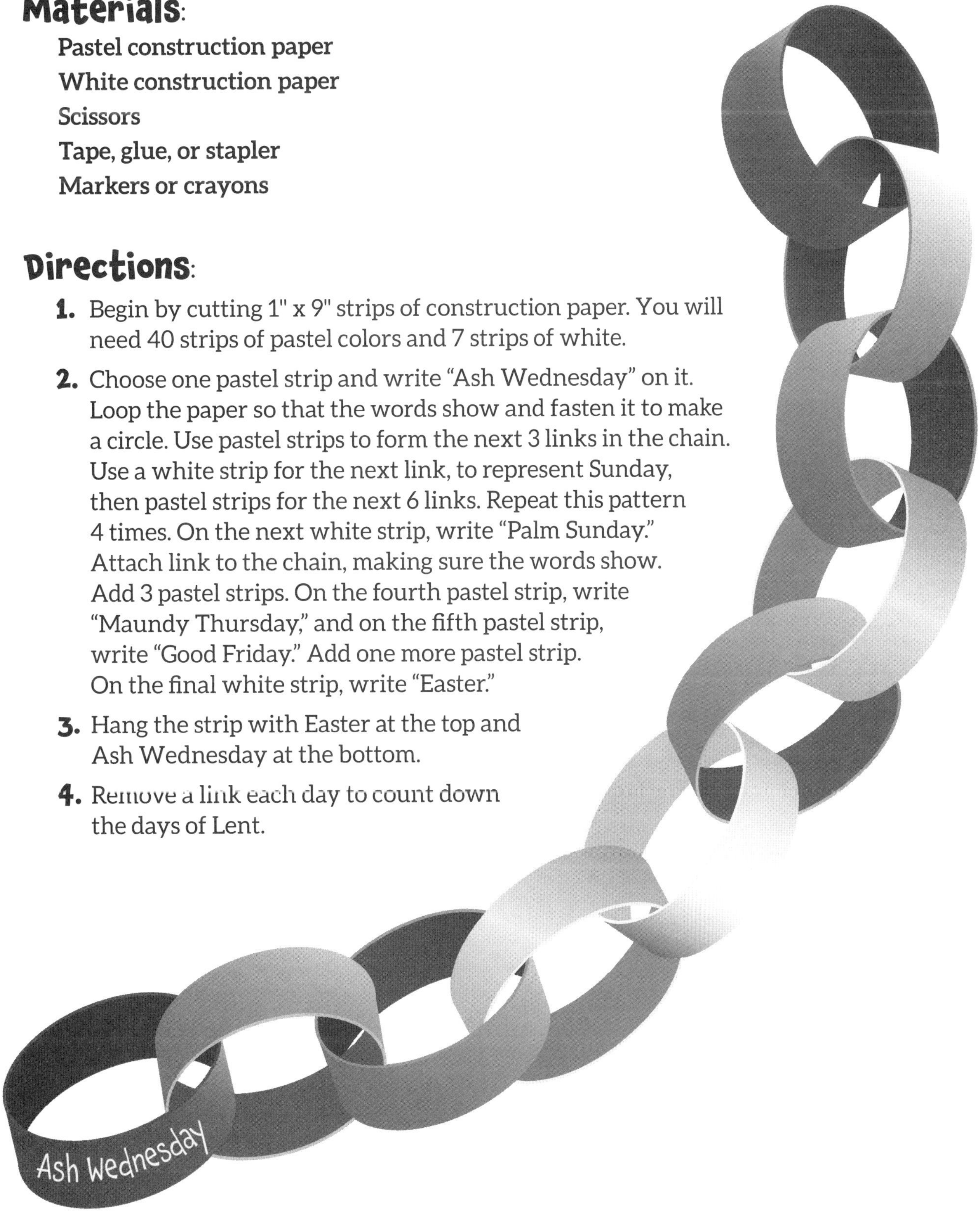

Palm Leaf Stamping Matthew 21:1–11

Blessed is he who comes in the name of the Lord!
Hosanna in the highest heaven!

MATTHEW 21:9 (NIV®)

Jesus and His disciples were on their way to Jerusalem for Passover. When they were almost there, Jesus sent two of the disciples ahead. "Go into the village, and you will find a donkey and her colt. Bring them to me. If anyone asks what you are doing, just tell them the Lord needs them."

When the disciples returned, they placed their cloaks over the donkey colt for Jesus to sit on. A very large crowd gathered and began laying their cloaks on the ground for Jesus to ride over. They also cut branches from the trees to cover the road.

The people treated Jesus like a king and made a loud and happy parade as He passed by. They shouted, "Hosanna!... Blessed is he who comes in the name of the Lord!" (Matthew 21:9, NIV®).

Questions:

1. Why were Jesus and His disciples going to Jerusalem?
2. Who did the people think Jesus was?
3. Have you ever gone to a parade? What did you see, hear, and do?
4. What would you shout if you saw Jesus riding by?

Try this craft to make a palm tree with branches like people may have waved to celebrate Jesus.

Materials:

9" x 12" pieces of construction paper in brown, green, gray, and blue
Glue
Green craft paint
Small paper plate
Small pieces of fabric (approximately 2–4" in length)
Soft kitchen sponge

Directions:

1. Choose a full sheet of blue construction paper for your background. Next cut a curvy line across a green piece of construction paper. That will be your ground. Glue into place. Then cut another piece in the shape of a road and glue on top of the green, leaving space for your palm tree.
2. Find the templates below and a make copy. Trace the tree trunk on the brown paper. Cut it out and glue it next to the road on the ground. Make sure to leave enough space at the top for the leaves.
3. Cut the sponge into a simple palm leaf shape using templates below.
4. Place a thin layer of green paint on a paper plate.
5. Dip the sponge into the paint and stamp leaves at the top of the tree trunk.
6. Reload the sponge with paint every other time you stamp.
7. Glue scraps of material below the tree on the road. These will resemble the cloaks people put on the ground for Jesus to ride over.

Palm leaves

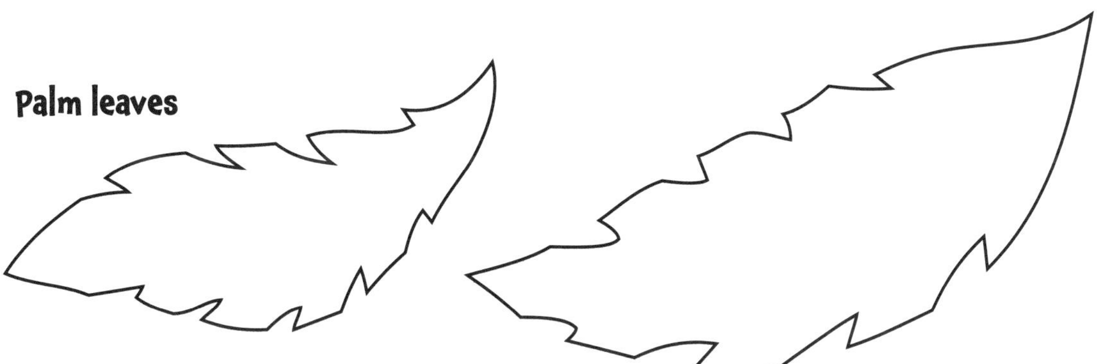

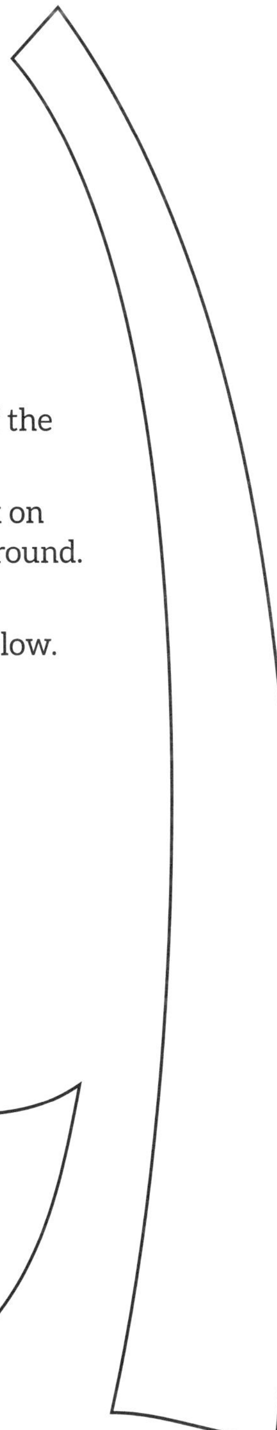

Tree trunk

Flower Garden

Revelation 21:3–5

"There will be no more death or mourning or crying or pain,
for the old order of things has passed away."
He who was seated on the throne said, "I am making everything new!"

REVELATION 21:4–5 (NIV®)

The colors of spring flowers are all around us, bringing joy to our hearts as they brighten our world. But before we could pick a flower, someone had to plant a seed. When you hold a seed in your hand, it doesn't look like much—most are small, brown, and dry. On the outside, a seed looks dead.

Then someone takes that seed and buries it in the ground. Things must seem pretty hopeless for the seed, down in the dark, damp earth. But the sun shines, and the rain falls...and pretty soon, a little shoot of green pokes above the ground. Before long, a beautiful flower stretches out its colorful petals, and a wonderful fragrance fills the air. New life has come!

Easter reminds us that because of Jesus, we can have a new life, too. Before we meet Jesus, our lives can seem like that dried up seed—sad and hopeless. But Jesus knows we have something very special inside, just waiting to bloom. When we ask Jesus to be our Savior, we get a fresh start. He gives us so much joy that it spills over to everyone around us!

Questions:

1. What is the first step to growing a flower?
2. Name three things a seed needs before it can grow.
3. How does Jesus give us a new life?
4. Who can you tell about Jesus?

Make this flower craft and then give it to someone you care about. Tell them the good news about Jesus!

Materials:

Tissue paper in multiple colors
Scissors
Pipe cleaners
Stapler

Directions:

1. Cut the stack of tissue paper in 8" squares. You will need at least 6-10 for each flower depending on how full you want it to be.
2. Stack 6-10 layers of tissue paper on top of each other with the edges lined up. You can use all of one color or layer multiple colors.
3. Start on one edge and fan-fold all of the layers together into 1" sections. Continue folding back and forth until all of the tissue is folded.
4. Staple the layers together exactly in the middle. Then tightly wrap a pipe cleaner around the center of the folded paper and secure by twisting together. Leave enough pipe cleaner on one end to make a stem. The folded edge should be facing up.
5. Using scissors, cut the ends on each side of the folded papers. You can experiment with different edges to create different shaped petals.
6. While holding by the pipe cleaner, spread out the folds and carefully lift up on each layer of tissue and fluff into the shape of a flower.

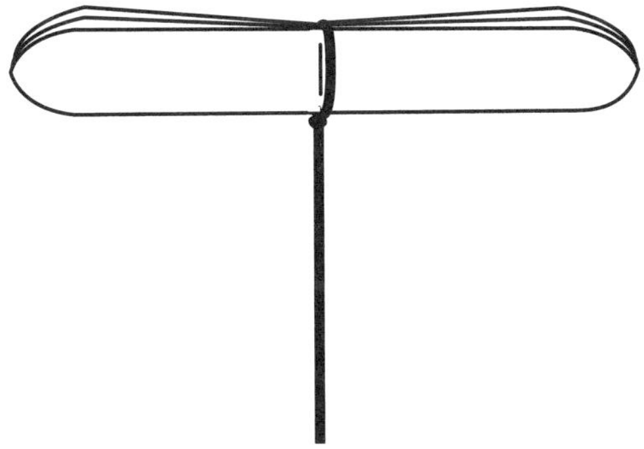

Easter Mosaic

John 3:1–21

For God so loved the world that he gave his one and only Son,
that whoever believes in him shall not perish but have eternal life.

JOHN 3:16 (NIV®)

Nicodemus was a Pharisee and a member of the Jewish ruling council. Most Pharisees did not like Jesus or His teaching, but Nicodemus wanted to get to know Jesus better. One night, he went to visit Jesus. Nicodemus said, "We can tell You have come from God because no one could do what You do without God."

Jesus wanted to teach Nicodemus about the kingdom of God and what it means to be "born again." We cannot be born again on our own or by following rules. We are born again by believing Jesus is God's Son. Jesus explained this by saying, "For God so loved the world that he gave his one and only Son, that whoever believes in him shall not perish but have eternal life" (John 3:16, NIV®).

When someone is born again, God's Spirit gives him or her a new life. We aren't born with a new body, but with a new spirit inside. When we believe in Jesus, He gives us that new spirit, so we can live forever with Him in heaven.

Questions:

1. How was Nicodemus different than other Pharisees?
2. Why do you think Nicodemus went to see Jesus at night?
3. How can a person be "born again"?
4. Have you made the decision to live for Jesus? Why or why not?
5. What do you think heaven will be like?

Now, make an Easter mosaic that represents new life—a cross, a lily, or a butterfly. Can you think of any other things that symbolize the new life we have because of Jesus?

Materials:

Heavy paper (like cardstock), cardboard, or thin plywood
Pattern to trace (cross, lily, butterfly, etc.)
Marker or pen
Glue
Small colorful objects such as seeds, cereal, eggshells, sugar, candy sprinkles, or construction paper cut up into small pieces.

Directions:

1. To begin, draw or trace your Easter design on heavy paper.
2. Working in one small section at a time, from top to bottom, apply glue to your design and sprinkle area with the small colorful objects of your choice. You may make your design more interesting by using a variety of small objects and different colors.
3. Press gently to make sure the objects stick to the glue.
4. Move on to the next section.
5. When the design is filled in, then a contrasting color can be used to fill in the background. If your design is in dark colors, a light-colored background will help it show up better and vice versa.
6. Lay your project flat and allow to dry thoroughly before hanging.

Washcloth Handprint

John 13:1–17

He poured water into a basin and began to wash his disciples' feet, drying them with the towel that was wrapped around him.

JOHN 13:5 (NIV®)

Jesus and His disciples were eating the Passover meal. Jesus got up from the table, wrapped a towel around His waist, and filled a large bowl with water. Then He knelt down and began washing His disciples' feet. The disciples were surprised. Usually a servant washed the guests' feet when they entered the house, not someone special like Jesus! They didn't understand why He would do such a thing.

When Jesus came to Peter, Peter said, "Jesus, You cannot wash my feet!"

Jesus said, "Peter, if I don't wash your feet, then you can't be part of Me."

Peter loved Jesus. He definitely wanted to do what Jesus wanted him to do. Peter said, "Then don't just wash my feet. Wash my hands and my head, too!"

Jesus explained that wasn't necessary. He told the disciples that He was giving them an example of what to do in the future. Just as Jesus served them by washing their feet, they should serve others, too. And, so should we.

Questions:

1. What did Jesus do for His disciples that they thought was strange?
2. Who usually washed a guest's feet?
3. Why do you think Peter did not want Jesus to wash his feet?
4. Why did Jesus give this example to the disciples?
5. How can you serve others today?

Make a special washcloth to remind you of how Jesus washed His disciples' feet.

Materials:

Fabric paint
Styrofoam plate
New washcloth
Foam paint brush

Directions:

1. Place the washcloth on a hard surface and make sure it has no wrinkles in it.
2. Pour some fabric paint on the Styrofoam plate and smear it around until the paint covers most of the plate.
3. Press your hand into the paint. Make sure every finger and the palm have paint on them. Use a foam paint brush to get rid of excess paint and to ensure even coverage.
4. Place your hand over the center of the washcloth and press your palm down into the washcloth. Before moving your hand, press on each finger to make sure the paint has transferred to the cloth. Lift your hand straight up so the paint will not smear. It might be helpful to have someone hold down the washcloth or tape it to the hard surface, so it doesn't stick to your hand.
5. Let dry completely before handling.

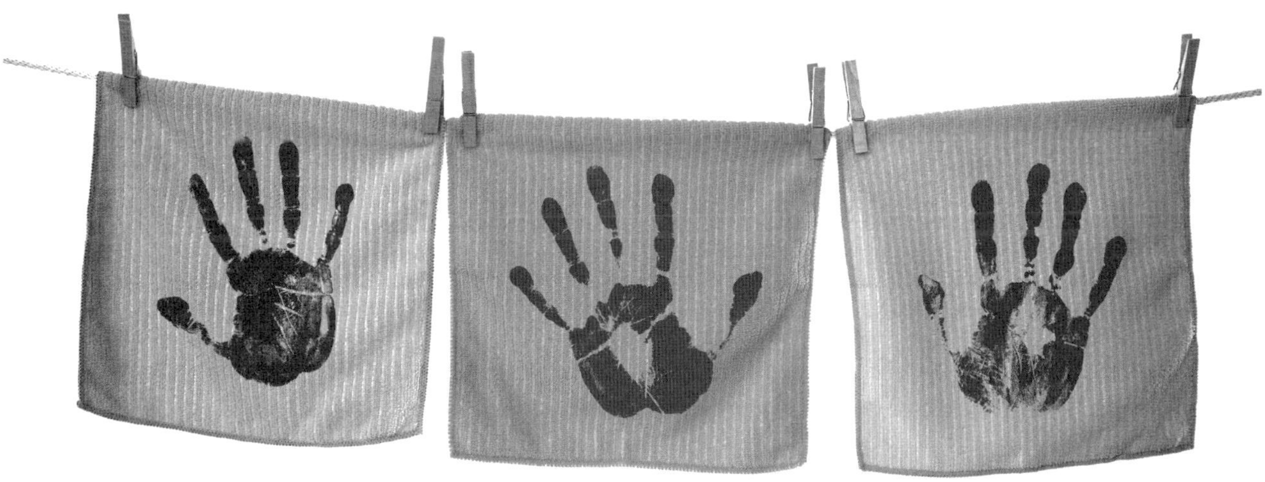

The Last Supper

Luke 22:7–30

When the hour came, Jesus and his apostles reclined at the table. And he said to them, "I have eagerly desired to eat this Passover with you before I suffer. For I tell you, I will not eat it again until it finds fulfillment in the kingdom of God."

LUKE 22:14–16 (NIV®)

The day had come to eat the Passover meal. Jews celebrate Passover to remember how God freed them from slavery in Egypt long ago. Jesus sent Peter and John to find a place in town to have the meal.

Jesus told them, "You will see a man carrying a water jar. Follow him to a house and say to the owner, 'The Teacher wants to know where the guest room is that will be used for the Passover meal with His disciples.' Then the owner will show you the large upper room that we will use." The disciples found everything just as Jesus said they would.

Later, Jesus and the disciples sat around the table. Jesus knew He would die soon and wanted to give His disciples a way to remember Him. Jesus took some bread and wine. He gave thanks, broke the bread, and gave them some, saying, "This is my body given for you; do this in remembrance of me" (Luke 22:19, NIV®). Then He took the cup and said, "This cup is the new covenant in my blood, which is poured out for you" (Luke 22:20, NIV®).

We call this meal the Last Supper because it was the last time Jesus ate with His disciples before He died. When we share the bread and wine (or grape juice) at church, we call this "communion." We remember all that Jesus did so that we can have eternal life with Him in heaven.

Questions:

1. What is Passover?
2. How do you think Jesus knew what the disciples would see in town before they got there?
3. Jews sacrificed animals as an offering to God, so their sins could be forgiven. When Jesus talked about the "new covenant in my blood," He meant that the blood He was going to shed on the cross would take away our sins from now on. How do you feel when you think about Jesus dying for your sins?
4. Have you ever taken communion at church? If you have, what does that mean to you?
5. Does your family have big meals or celebrations together? What is that like? When the disciples and Jesus ate together, what do you think they did?

Make this Last Supper craft to help you imagine what it would be like to sit at the table with Jesus.

Materials:

2 Egg cartons	Brown paper lunch sack	7 Jumbo craft sticks
Glue or tape	Markers/Colored Pencils	Stapler
Scissors	Hobby knife	2 - 3 oz. paper cups

Directions:

1. Begin by cutting off the lids from both egg cartons and set aside. Turn the carton over so the bumps face up. Overlap the last two bumps from each of the egg cartons to make one long carton. Cut slits between the last two egg slots on one side so that the top carton can fit together tightly. See **Figure A** on page 44. These are the seats for Jesus and His disciples. Secure together with glue or staples.
2. Using the hobby knife, cut horizontal slits on the bottom on 13 bumps for the craft sticks to slide into. You need to do this to one entire row of the carton, and only one front bump on each end. Refer to **Figure A** on page 44. The remaining bumps will be used to hold one side of the table.
3. To make the table, cut off one end of each of the two lids. Overlap the cut ends and slide together to form a table. Use the uncut bumps as a guide to determine the length. Staple together to make it secure. See **Figure B** on page 44.
4. Glue two paper cups in the corners of the front side of the table. You can staple them to the side of the egg carton lid for additional strength. These are the legs of the outside of the table.
5. Open a small brown paper lunch bag and notice the folds on the long sides of the bag. Cut the bag in half using the fold lines as a guide. Slide the two halves together to form a tablecloth. Adjust to fit and secure with glue or tape.
6. Make a photocopy of pages 44-45 on paper or cardstock. Color Jesus, the disciples, and the tableware with colored pencils or markers. Carefully cut them out.
7. Cut 7 jumbo craft sticks in half and glue them to the backs of Jesus and the disciples. The sticks should extend past the edge of the paper, so they can be placed in the carton seats. Write the names of the disciples on the back of the craft sticks. See **Figure C** on page 44.
8. Place Jesus and the disciples into their slots. Lower the table in place onto the open bumps. Set the tableware on the table. Try to memorize all of the names of the disciples that were with Jesus at the Last Supper.

Prayer Eggs

John 17:1–26

After Jesus said this, he looked toward heaven and prayed.

JOHN 17:1 (NIV®)

Jesus knew the time was coming soon when He would die on the cross. He tried to prepare His disciples for what was about to happen, but they couldn't really understand. After He had taught them and shared the Passover meal with them, Jesus prayed.

First, He prayed for Himself. Jesus had spent His life on earth to bring God glory. His purpose was to show people the way to receive eternal life and know the one true God. Jesus said He had finished the work God had given Him to do. Soon, Jesus would be going back to God, where He was before the world began.

Next, Jesus prayed for His disciples. He talked to God about how the disciples had learned from Him and obeyed God's Word. Jesus knew He wouldn't be in the world anymore, but that His disciples would. He prayed they would be unified—working together, loving God and each other, and sharing one purpose. Jesus prayed that God would give them joy and protect them from the devil. He asked God to help them as they shared the good news about Jesus with the world.

Finally, Jesus prayed for people like us, who would believe in Jesus long after He was gone from the world. He prayed we would be strong in our faith, so we can be an example to people around us, and they will come to believe in Jesus, too. Jesus promised to continue to help us know about God, to work together as one, and to experience His love.

Questions:

1. What did Jesus do for the disciples before He died?
2. What three things did Jesus pray about?
3. Which of the things Jesus prayed about surprises you the most? Why?
4. Who do you pray for? What do you hope God will do for that person?
5. Why should we pray?

These Easter prayer eggs will help you to get in the habit of praying every day. Our prayers to God are very important. Besides the things listed below, what else would you like to pray about?

Materials:

Colorful lunch or gift bag
6 slips of paper to write prayers on
Crayons or markers
Pencil
6 plastic eggs

Directions:

1. Using the 6 slips of paper, write the following prayers on each one:
    - Dear Father, I don't want to act like I'm ashamed to be one of Your followers. Help me not to be afraid when others ask me about You.
    - Dear Father, I want to give with a cheerful heart, and I want to give You everything. That's what You deserve.
    - Dear Father, help me to bear fruit and be all that You created me to be. I want others to know more about You because of how I live and what I say.
    - Dear Father, help me to love others as much as I love myself. No, Father, help me to love them MORE than I love myself. It will take Your strength to do that. You can remind me when I'm being selfish and when I need to think of others more.
    - Dear Father, if I had a palm branch, I would wave it and shout, "Hosanna!" I want to celebrate Your gift to me every day of my life. Hosanna to my King!
    - Dear Father, help me to remember what You did for me when You sent Your Son, Jesus, to die on the cross and rise from the grave. When I see or taste the bread and juice, I will stop all my other thoughts and be thankful.
2. Roll each strip of paper around a pencil so it will fit in the egg easier. Place one prayer inside each egg.
3. Decorate the bag with Easter decorations. Store your eggs in the lunch bag.
4. Each day pull out an egg and read the prayer on the paper. This is only a starter prayer. Each prayer has something to do with one of the stories that occurred during Holy Week.
5. Put the prayer slip back in the egg and return it to your bag when you are finished praying. You can use your prayer eggs over and over again.

Crown of Thorns

John 18:28—19:16 and 1 Peter 5:4

The soldiers twisted together a crown of thorns and put it on his head.

JOHN 19:2 (NIV®)

Pilate was the Roman governor. Jewish leaders took Jesus to him to be judged. At first, Pilate didn't want to have anything to do with the situation. Pilate knew Jesus had done nothing wrong, but the Jews kept pressuring him to convict Jesus of a crime. Pilate asked Jesus, "Are You the king of the Jews?" Jesus replied, "My kingdom is not of this world" (from John 18:33–36, NIV®).

Pilate sent Jesus away to be beaten. Soldiers twisted together a crown of thorns and pushed it down on Jesus' head. They made Him wear a purple robe like a king would wear. Then they hit Jesus and mocked Him.

Later, Pilate talked to the Jewish leaders again. He said, "I cannot find any crime this man has committed." But the Jewish leaders insisted that they wanted Jesus to be crucified. Finally, Pilate gave in and sent Jesus away to be killed. He cared more about keeping peace among the people than he cared about truth and justice.

Questions:

1. What was Pilate's job?
2. Why didn't Pilate want to judge Jesus' case?
3. What did the soldiers do to make Jesus like a king?
4. How are people supposed to treat a king? How did the soldiers treat Jesus?
5. Why did Pilate hand Jesus over to be killed?

Because Jesus wore a crown of thorns, we will one day receive a heavenly crown (see 1 Peter 5:4). This craft will help you remember the two kinds of crowns.

Materials:

Small grapevine wreath
Wooden toothpicks
Colored rhinestones
Glue

Directions:

Note: If you have real grapevines available where you live, ask an adult to help you make a wreath out of one. If not, then grapevine wreaths can be purchased at most department stores and craft and hobby stores. Usually they are found in the store's floral department.

1. Place the grapevine wreath flat on a table. Think about some ways you have disobeyed God—how you have sinned. Take a toothpick and wedge it down into the weave of the grapevine. Continue until you have several toothpicks sticking out to resemble Jesus' crown of thorns. As you look at the "thorns," think about this: Jesus took all of this punishment—the cross and the thorny crown—so that we could be with God forever. When we claim and accept Jesus' sacrifice, we get the promise of being with God forever in heaven.
2. Turn the grapevine over. Imagine what heaven will be like. Fill in the blanks: Heaven will have no more ____________________. Heaven will be ____________________. Next, glue some colored rhinestone jewels in place around the circle of the crown. When you are finished, look at how beautiful the colors are on this side of the crown. The Bible tells us that Jesus has gone to get a place ready for us, and that we will have a heavenly crown.
3. When the glue on your project is dry, flip the crown from front to back and look at the thorns and jewels. Think about the crown of thorns Jesus wore. Each thorn represents how we have hurt God. The jewels remind us of the crown we will wear in heaven because Jesus wore the thorny crown.

Cock-a-doodle Rooster Luke 22:31–34, 54–62

Jesus answered, "I tell you, Peter, before the rooster crows today, you will deny three times that you know me."

LUKE 22:34 (NIV®)

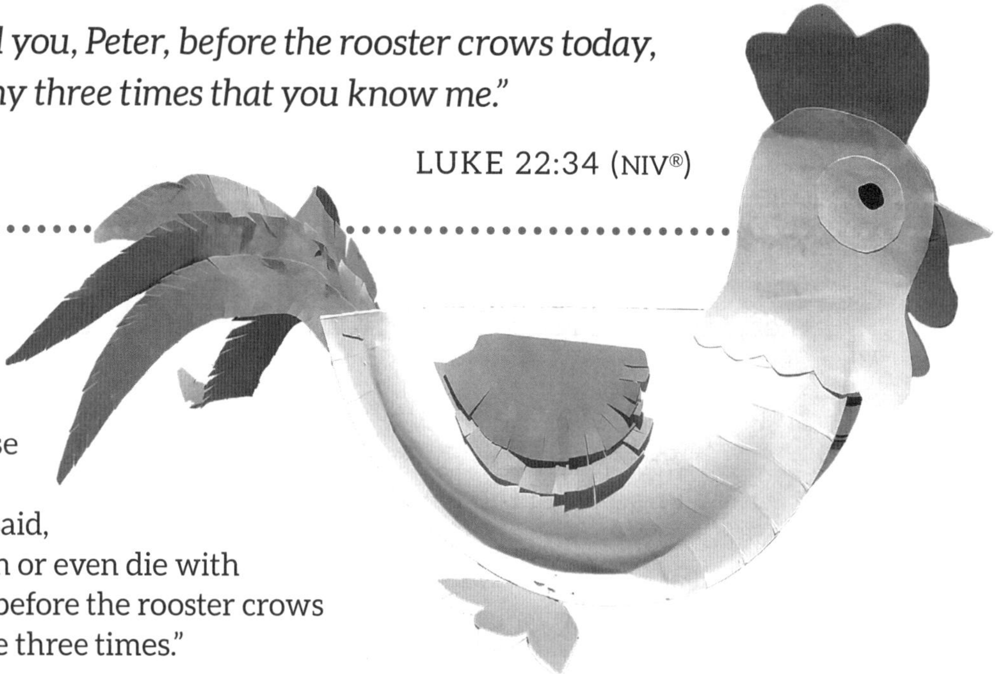

After the Last Supper, Jesus talked to Peter. Jesus said He had prayed for Peter because Peter was going to turn away from Him. Peter said, "Jesus, I will go to prison or even die with you." Jesus said, "Peter, before the rooster crows today, you will deny Me three times."

Later, Jesus was taken away to be judged. Peter followed at a distance. He saw some people had made a fire in the courtyard, so he joined them to wait. A servant girl saw Peter and recognized him. She said, "This man was with Jesus." Peter said, "I don't even know the man."

A little later, someone else saw Peter and said, "You are one of Jesus' followers." Again, Peter said, "No, I'm not!" Finally, a man said, "This fellow was with Jesus. He is from Galilee." Peter answered, "I have no idea what you are talking about!"

Just then, the rooster crowed. Peter remembered what Jesus had said, and he knew that he had disowned Jesus three times. He was so sorry for what he had done that he went away and cried.

Questions:

1. Why did Jesus pray for Peter?
2. When Peter denied Jesus three times, what happened?
3. Why do you think Peter said he didn't know Jesus?
4. How do you think Jesus felt when He knew His close friend, Peter, was going to say he didn't know Him?
5. Have you ever told a lie when you were afraid? What was it? Why did you do that?

Jesus loved Peter and understood why Peter denied Him.
Jesus knows we are human beings and that we are afraid sometimes.
Let's make a rooster craft to help us remember the story.

Materials:

Construction paper	Paper plate	Glue or tape
Stapler	Scissors	Markers, crayons, or paint

Directions:

1. Flip the paper plate so the bottom is facing you. Color it whatever color you like or leave it white. This will be the body of your rooster.
2. Fold the paper plate in half with the colored side out. Cut a 1 inch slit on one end of the fold for the tail feathers to slide into.
3. Use the templates on page 46 to draw the rooster parts on some colorful construction paper. Cut out the parts following the instructions on the template. Cut small slits around the tail and wings to make fringe for feathers. There should be at least 4 wings, 5 tail feathers, 2 heads, and 2 eyes.
4. Glue or tape the beak, comb, and wattle (the red dangly thing on a rooster's neck under the beak) on one side of the head. Glue or tape the heads together leaving the neck part open to slide over the plate. Place one eye on each side of the head. Slide the head over one corner of the plate so each side of the neck is showing. Once you have it in place, tape or staple the head on to the rooster's body.
5. Glue or tape 2 or more wings to each side of the rooster's body so that you can see both layers. Layer at least 5 tail feathers together like a pony tail and staple them at one end. Slide the fixed tail end into the slit of the plate and make sure it is in far enough in to be supported. Staple the tail in place.
6. To attach the feet, first bend the rounded edge back slightly on each side where the plate touches the table. That is where the feet will be attached. Staple one foot at a time to the edge you just bent. The strip between the feet will keep the plate in place and make it easier to stand.

Standing Cross

Luke 23:26–43

When they came to the place called the Skull, they crucified him there.... Jesus said, "Father, forgive them, for they do not know what they are doing."

LUKE 23:33–34 (NIV®)

Being killed on a cross was a terrible way to die. The Romans used this method because it was very painful and humiliating for the victim. They crucified people who were criminals, a threat to the government, or an enemy of their country.

Jesus was crucified because the religious leaders of the time felt threatened by His popularity and the truth He taught about God. Jesus never committed a single crime or sin, yet God had planned for Him to die to save us from our sins. When God gave the Law to Moses, He said an animal had to be sacrificed for people to be forgiven of their sins. People had to sacrifice animals again and again whenever they sinned. But when Jesus' life was sacrificed, our sins were taken away once and for all. Never again would a person have to sacrifice an animal to receive God's forgiveness.

Every person who believes in Jesus can be forgiven of their sins. All we have to do is confess what we have done wrong and ask Him to forgive us. The cross where Jesus died has become a symbol of hope for Christians. Because Jesus died, we can live forever!

Questions:

1. What method did the Romans use to kill people?
2. Why was Jesus an unusual choice for death on a cross?
3. According to God's Law, what did someone have to do to be forgiven for their sins?
4. How can we be forgiven for our sins now?
5. Have you asked Jesus to forgive you for the wrong things you have done? How did you feel afterwards?

Make this cross craft to remember the gift of forgiveness we have because Jesus gave His life for us.

Materials:

Jumbo craft sticks
Hot glue gun or craft glue
Styrofoam ice cream cup
Hobby knife
Green tissue paper
Purple or white ribbon
Silk flowers (optional)
Tape

Directions:

1. Make one craft stick shorter by drawing a curve using another stick, and then cut it with scissors. This will be the crossbeam. Use craft glue or a hot glue gun to attach them together. Set aside to dry.
2. Cut the green tissue paper into a little less than 1" squares.
3. Turn the Styrofoam cup upside down so the flat bottom is facing up. This will be the ground that the cross goes into. Carefully make a slit in the bottom of the cup with a hobby knife as wide as the craft stick. This is where the cross will be placed.
4. Wad up individual pieces of tissue paper and glue them onto the cup. Completely cover the outside of the cup.
5. Poke the base of the cross through the center of the bottom of the cup so the cross is upright.
6. Take a piece of purple or white ribbon and drape it over the crossbeam of the cross. Glue it in a couple of places so it won't fall off.
7. Add flowers at the base of the cross by first poking a hole through the cup with a pencil, then pushing the stem of the flower through. Secure the stem with tape or glue on the inside of the cup.

7 Last Words of Jesus on the Cross Book

Even when Jesus was dying on the cross, He was thinking of others. The Bible tells us about seven things Jesus said from the cross. Jesus was in terrible pain, and it was very difficult for Him to speak at all. That fact makes these statements even more important for us to remember and think about.

While He was on the cross, Jesus forgave the very men who were crucifying Him. He also forgave the thief who was crucified next to Him when he asked Jesus to remember Him. Jesus saw His mother and made sure she would be cared for by His disciple, John.

Jesus was carrying the weight of the sins of the whole world as He died. At one point, He cried out to God, "Why have You forsaken Me?" Jesus said He was thirsty. Finally, His suffering came to an end. He said, "It is finished," and committed His Spirit into God's hands. Then Jesus died.

Questions:

1. Why is it important to remember what Jesus said when He was on the cross?
2. Who did Jesus forgive?
3. What family member did Jesus mention?
4. What did Jesus ask God?
5. If you knew you were going to heaven, what would your last words be?

7 last words from the cross:

1. *"Father, forgive them, for they do not know what they are doing."* Luke 23:34 (NIV®)
2. *"Truly I tell you, today you will be with me in paradise."* Luke 23:43 (NIV®)
3. *"Woman, here is your son," and to the disciple, "Here is your mother."* John 19:26–27 (NIV®)
4. *"My God, my God, why have you forsaken me?"* Matthew 27:46, Mark 15:34 (NIV®)
5. *"I am thirsty."* John 19:28 (NIV®)
6. *"It is finished."* John 19:30(NIV®)
7. *"Father, into your hands I commit my spirit."* Luke 23:46 (NIV®)

Make a book to help you remember the last words of Jesus.

Materials:

1 sheet of construction paper or card stock
4 sheets of white paper
Markers, crayons, pen, pencil
Ruler
Hole punch
Ribbon, yarn, shoe lace, etc.

Directions:

1. Fold the piece of construction paper and the 4 pieces of white paper in half. Your book can be any size you like. Just make sure the construction paper and the white paper are the same size.
2. Stack all of the papers together and fold. Put the folded book on a flat surface. Place a ruler along the folded edge and use a pencil to lightly draw a line down the front of the book.
3. With the paper still folded, use a hole punch to make an even row of holes down the side of the book between the fold and the pencil line you drew. Space the holes about an inch apart.
4. Use ribbon or another kind of string to tie your book together. You can use a short string to tie a bow through each hole or use a long string to start at the top and sew your book together. Don't forget to tie or knot or bow, so your string doesn't come loose.
5. On the cover of your book, write the title: **7 Last Words of Jesus on the Cross**. Decorate the cover with your own drawings or stickers however you like.
6. Open the book to the first page. Draw an Easter picture here.
7. On the next 2 pages, draw a picture on the left. On the right, write the first words Jesus said on the cross. You will find them listed on page 24.
8. Continue through the book, drawing a picture on the left and writing the words of Jesus on the right.
9. On the last page, write a prayer or your thoughts about what Jesus' death on the cross means to you.

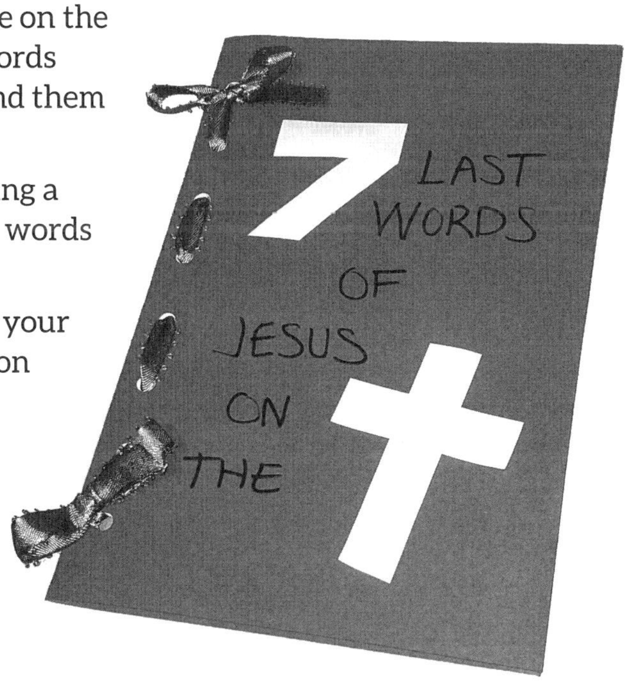

Scented Play Dough

John 19:38–42

Nicodemus brought a mixture of myrrh and aloes, about seventy-five pounds. Taking Jesus' body, the two of them wrapped it, with the spices, in strips of linen

JOHN 19:39–40 (NIV®)

Name some spices that you have in your kitchen cabinets. Why do we use spices? In Bible times, people used many of these same spices to put on a body for burial. They didn't have funeral directors who embalmed the body, so they would put both liquid and powder spices on them.

The Bible tells us in John 19:39–40 (NIV®) that Nicodemus, a Jewish leader who believed in Jesus, brought 75 pounds of myrrh and aloes to put on Jesus' dead body. In those days, the more spices that were used in the burial, the more honored and respected the person was. A typical amount of spices for an honored person might be 40 pounds. An average person would have been buried with much less. Obviously, Nicodemus really loved and respected Jesus.

Questions:

1. What did Nicodemus bring for Jesus' burial?
2. How could you tell if a person was more respected or less?
3. What can you do to honor Jesus?

Cinnamon gives this play dough a nice fragrance.
Remember Jesus as you mold objects out of the dough.

Materials:

- Cinnamon
- Cream of tartar
- Flour
- Measuring spoon and cups
- Salt
- Saucepan
- Vegetable oil
- Water
- Waxed paper or plastic table cloth
- Wooden spatula

To make the play dough:

Recipe for Cinnamon Play Dough

- ¾ cup salt
- 1 ½ cup flour
- 3 tablespoons vegetable oil
- 1 ½ teaspoons cream of tartar
- 1 ½ cup water
- 2 tablespoons cinnamon

Mix well until dough forms. The cinnamon will naturally color the play dough a reddish-brown.

Directions:

1. Make the play dough using the recipe listed above.
2. Put down a piece of waxed paper or plastic table cloth to protect your work surface.
3. Use the play dough to create an Easter scene. You could make the tomb and stone, the bread and cup Jesus and the disciples used at the Last Supper, and/or a bowl and water pitcher like Jesus used to wash the disciples' feet. Use your imagination to think up other things to make.

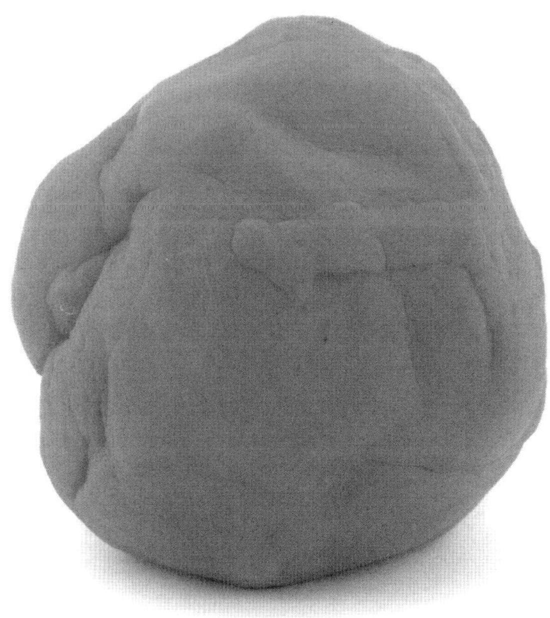

Potpourri Ornament

Mark 16:1–8

When the Sabbath was over, Mary Magdalene, Mary the mother of James, and Salome bought spices so that they might go to anoint Jesus' body.

MARK 16:1 (NIV®)

When Jesus died, His body was covered in spices and wrapped in linen cloth. People preserved dead bodies with spices in those days to help cover up the smell of decay.

After the Sabbath, the women who followed Jesus brought spices to put on Jesus' body. Just like we bring flowers to someone's grave when we visit it, people brought spices to honor Jesus. The women were shocked to discover that their spices would not be needed. Jesus was no longer in the tomb! Instead, they saw an angel who told them Jesus had risen to life again!

Questions:

1. Why did people put spices on dead bodies?
2. Why didn't the women get to use their spices?
3. How can you show someone special that you honor them while they are still living?

Create a potpourri ornament to remind you of the spices the women brought to Jesus' tomb.

Materials:

Plastic table covering
Ruler or dowel rod
Bowl
Potpourri
Small round balloon
Packing tape
Liquid starch
Glue gun
2 buckets
Pastel yarns
Scissors
Ribbon (optional)

Directions:

1. Cover the work surface with a plastic table covering.
2. Blow up the balloon to the size you want your ornament. (You could also use a water balloon.)
3. Turn your buckets over and rest the ruler between them. Tape the ruler down with packing tape to add stability.
4. Tie one end of a piece of yarn around the neck of the balloon and the other end around the ruler, so the balloon is hanging between the buckets.
5. Cut the rest of the yarn for this project into manageable lengths (about 30"- 45").
6. Put a good amount of the liquid starch in a bowl. Pull the yarn through the liquid starch until the entire piece of yarn is wet. Then wrap it around the balloon. Keep wrapping pieces of yarn around the balloon until there are just small holes showing through to the balloon.
7. Let the balloon hang overnight. You want the yarn to be completely dry, so let it hang longer if you need to.
8. When the yarn is dry, gently pop the balloon. Choose a point on the balloon to be the top of your ornament. Clip a piece of yarn, or two if necessary, to make a hole big enough to get the balloon out.
9. Through that same hole, poke pieces of potpourri.
10. Once the ornament is about half-full of potpourri, use the hot glue gun to glue the clipped ends of yarn back together.
11. Make a hanger out of a piece of yarn or some ribbon.
12. Hang your potpourri ornament where its sweet smell will fill the room.

Easter Painting on Glass

Luke 23: 50–54, 24:1–8

They found the stone rolled away from the tomb, but when they entered, they did not find the body of the Lord Jesus.

LUKE 24:2–3 (NIV®)

Joseph of Arimathea was a good man. He was a member of the Jewish Council, but he did not agree with the others that Jesus should be killed. After Jesus died, Joseph went to Pilate and asked for Jesus' body. He took it down off the cross, wrapped it in linen, and put it in a new tomb that had been cut from the rock. No one else had ever been buried there. The women who were Jesus' followers saw where Jesus was buried and went home to get spices ready to put on His body.

On the first day of the week, some women went back to the tomb. They were shocked to see that the stone had been rolled away. They looked inside, and Jesus' body wasn't there. They couldn't understand it! Who would have taken Jesus' body away?

While they were wondering about it, two men in clothes that shone like lightning appeared. They asked, "Why are you looking for the living where the dead are found? Jesus is not here. He has risen! Remember how He told you He would be raised on the third day?"

The women left the tomb and hurried to tell the disciples what had happened. Peter ran to the tomb and saw the strips of linen Jesus' body had been wrapped in, but Jesus was not there. He wondered what could have happened.

Questions:

1. Who was Joseph of Arimathea?
2. What was special about the tomb?
3. Why were the women shocked when they went back to the tomb?
4. Where was Jesus?
5. What would you think if you went to the tomb and Jesus was missing?

Use your creativity to paint a special picture of the tomb where Jesus was buried.

Materials:

- Picture frame with glass in it
- Construction paper
- Aluminum foil
- Craft or poster paint
- Paintbrush
- Small artificial flowers
- Glue

Directions:

1. Take apart the picture frame. Using the backer board or glass as a template, trace out the background on a piece of construction paper.
2. Layer more colors of construction paper to make the sun, grass and even a cross.
3. Next, tear off a piece of aluminum foil about the size of your frame. Crumple it up and then gently spread it out smooth. Cut out the shape of a tomb. If you need help, you can draw the tomb on paper, cut it out, and trace the shape onto your aluminum foil with a marker. Cut out the tomb, position it in the center of the picture, and glue it into place on your background.
4. Choose several small artificial flowers and glue them into place around the tomb.
5. Now place the glass from the frame over your tomb picture. With a paintbrush and black or gray paint, paint the stone for the door of the tomb onto the glass. Paint white clouds in the sky. Let it dry.
6. Flip the glass, paint side down, and put the picture frame back together.

Easter Egg Planter

Romans 6:4–5

Just as Christ was raised from the dead through the glory of the Father, we too may live a new life.

ROMANS 6:4 (NIV®)

When spring returns, we celebrate the new life we see all around us. Beautiful flowers bloom, the trees and grass turn green, and the birds come back. After the cold days and gray skies of winter, we enjoy the warmth and sunshine of spring.

Easter is a celebration of new life, too. At Easter, we remember how the sky turned dark when Jesus died. Jesus' friends were heartbroken that the One they loved so much was gone. They knew His body was in a cold, dark tomb. But just three days later, Jesus was alive again! Jesus' friends were overjoyed and began to share the good news with everyone.

When we believe in Jesus, we have hope. Jesus promised that everyone who believes in Him, even though we die here on earth, will live again in heaven. That is some good news worth celebrating!

Questions:

1. What is your favorite thing about spring?
2. Have you ever been to a funeral or known someone who has died? How did you feel?
3. Did Jesus' friends expect Him to come back to life again? Where did they think they would see Him again?
4. Whom will you tell the good news about Jesus?

When you make your Easter egg planter, think about how the egg is like a tomb, but the flower it holds is an example of new life.

Materials:

Eggshells (with only the top broken out)
Easter egg dye or watercolors
Tiny plants or artificial flowers
Soil
Strip of cardboard (approximately 1" x 5")

Directions:

1. Break a hole in the top of an eggshell, large enough to pour out the egg and for your finger to poke in. Rinse and let air dry.
2. Paint or dye shells.
3. When dry, fill with soil and press a flower or tiny plant into the soil.
4. Cut a thin strip of cardboard and write "Jesus Is Risen!" on it. Then tape or staple it together to form a circle. Set the egg planter in the cardboard circle to hold it upright.

Easter Angel

Matthew 28:1–7

An angel of the Lord came down from heaven and, going to the tomb, rolled back the stone and sat on it. His appearance was like lightning, and his clothes were white as snow.

MATTHEW 28:2–3 (NIV®)

Jesus' friends were so sad that He was dead. His body was buried in a tomb with a huge stone blocking the entrance. Mary and Mary Magdalene were taking spices to put on Jesus' body, but they didn't know how they would move the stone. It was way too heavy for them.

Suddenly, there was an earthquake. A bright angel dressed in white appeared and rolled away the stone and sat on it! The tomb guards were so frightened that they fainted. The women were afraid, too.

Then the angel spoke to them. He said, "I know you are looking for Jesus. He is not here. He has risen! Go and tell the disciples the good news. Let them know that they will see Jesus soon." The women were still scared, but they were also filled with joy. They ran quickly to tell the disciples that Jesus was alive!

Questions:

1. Who do you think the women expected to help them roll away the stone?
2. Who actually rolled away the stone?
3. How did the women feel when they saw the angel?
4. What would you do if an angel appeared in your room?
5. What question would you like to ask an angel?

Now, make an Easter angel to help you remember the angel the women saw at Jesus' tomb.

Materials:

- Paper plate or card stock
- Glitter
- Glue or tape
- Pipe cleaner
- Scissors
- Fine line black marker or black ink pen
- Markers
- Cotton balls

Directions:

1. Find the template on page 47 and make copies on card stock or trace on a paper plate. Carefully cut out the angel and the slits for assembly.
2. Along the rounded bottom edge, use a black pen to write, "He is not here; he has risen" (Matthew 28:6, NIV®).
3. Fold the arms down at the shoulder and slightly bend at the elbows so they are in front of the angel. Draw on a face and decorate the angel's robe with glitter, markers, or paper punches.
4. Flip the angel over and decorate the wings. When assembled, the wings will face forward.
5. Tear a piece of the cotton for the angel's hair and glue to the top of head. Make a halo from the pipe cleaner and tape or glue to the back of the head.
6. When the angel is dry, carefully form the robe into a cone, and slide the two slits together. Adjust the wings until they are in the correct place and tape or glue to secure.

Crystal Borax Ornament Acts 2:22–24

You…put him to death by nailing him to the cross.
But God raised him from the dead.

ACTS 2:23–24 (NIV®)

After Jesus died and rose to life again, Peter began to speak more and more about Jesus and who He was. Peter explained the scriptures that revealed the truth that Jesus was the promised Messiah—the One God had sent to save people from their sins.

Peter talked to the people about all the miracles Jesus had done that proved He was God's Son. He reminded them of how Jesus was killed on the cross and how God raised Him to life again. Because of his testimony, many people began to believe in Jesus and their lives were changed. They said they were sorry for their sins, and Peter baptized them.

Questions:

1. What did Peter do after Jesus died and rose to life?
2. What did Jesus come to do for everyone?
3. When the people heard what Peter said, what did they do?
4. What did the people do to show their lives were changed?
5. How is your life different because you know Jesus?

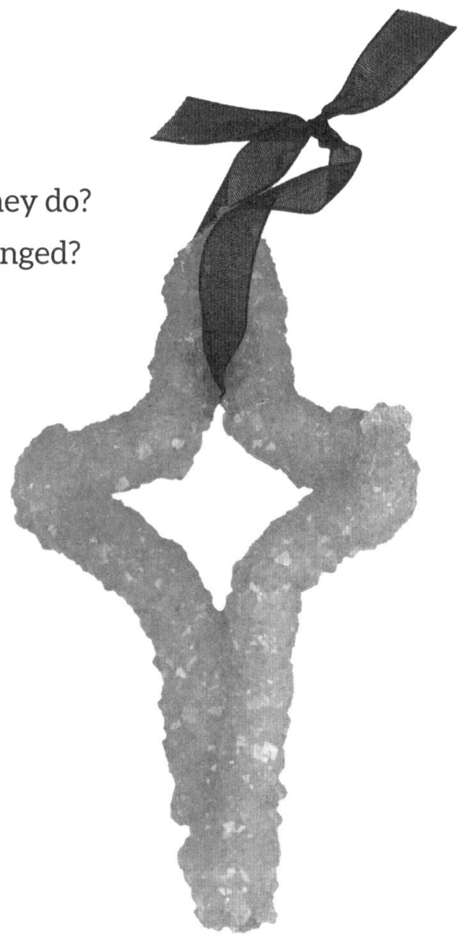

Just like Jesus transforms us by taking away our old, sinful life and giving us a fresh new start, this craft will transform an old pipe cleaner into something new. Try it out and see what happens!

Materials:

White chenille pipe cleaner
Dental floss, fishing line, or thin wire
New pencil or a piece of dowel rod
Wide-mouth jar
Tape
Borax
Boiling water
Food coloring
Thin ribbon

Directions:

Note: Borax is found in the detergent aisle of the grocery store. It is very important that your jar has a wide mouth and is also deep enough for the shape formed by the pipe cleaner to be completely submerged.

1. Twist the pipe cleaner into the shape of a cross. Twist the ends together securely, and then push them down flat so they are not sticking out.
2. Test the shape to make sure it will fit through the mouth of the jar without mashing it or changing the shape. If it doesn't fit, you either need a jar with a wider mouth, or you need to make your shape a little smaller.
3. Tie one end of a piece of dental floss to the pipe cleaner. Tie the other end to a pencil or dowel rod. Before going any further, set the dowel rod across the mouth of the jar and see how far the shape hangs in the jar. You don't want the shape to touch the bottom, but you also want it to be able to be covered with the mixture you'll make in the next step. You can adjust the length of the dental floss by rolling it around the dowel rod. Once you get it adjusted, place a piece of tape across the dental floss to hold it in place. Now take everything out of the jar and set it aside.
4. Pour boiling water into the jar until it is almost full, measuring the water as you go. Add 4 tablespoons of Borax for each cup of water in the jar and then stir, stir, stir! If all the Borax is dissolving, then you need to add some more. You know you have enough Borax when it will no longer dissolve in the boiling water.
5. If you leave the water like this, you will have a clear crystal ornament. Stir in some food coloring to make a colored ornament.
6. Now lower the cross shape into the jar and rest the dowel rod across the top of the jar. Make sure your pipe cleaner shape is completely submerged.
7. Set the jar in a place where it will not be bumped. The crystallization starts within the first hour, and if moved after that, even slightly, the process will be interrupted and will change what your ornament was supposed to look like.
8. Let the jar sit for 18–24 hours. You can watch it during that time, BUT DO NOT TOUCH!
9. Gently lift the dowel rod and pull the cross out of the water. It's quite a bit heavier now, isn't it?
10. Clip the dental floss from the ornament and add a loop of ribbon to use as a hanger.

Giant Egg Piñata

Romans 5:1–8

God's love has been poured out into our hearts through the Holy Spirit, who has been given to us.

ROMANS 5:5 (NIV®)

When we think about Easter and what Jesus did for us on the cross, we may wonder why Jesus gave up His life for people like us. He never sinned in His whole life, and yet He was willing to die for our sins. Why would He do that? Because He loved us and wanted us to be saved from hell.

When we believe in Jesus, our life is filled with peace. That doesn't mean we never have a problem, but we know that Jesus is always with us and will help us. We persevere in hard times—that means we keep trying and don't give up. We become people of character. We learn, grow, and become better people because of the hope Jesus gives us.

Paul wrote in a letter to the Romans about the love God has "poured" into our hearts. God proved how much He loved us when He sent Jesus, His only Son, to die in our place. That's a lot of love!

Questions:

1. Why did Jesus die for our sins?
2. What are some good things that happen when we believe in Jesus?
3. How do we know God loves us?
4. What can you do to show God how much you love Him?

Make a piñata, and when the candy pours out,
think about how that is like God's love pouring out on us.
Tell your friends about Jesus and what He did for us!

Materials:

Plastic table covering
Dowel rod
String
Large balloon
Newspaper
White paper
White glue
Disposable bowl or plastic container
Craft paints or tissue paper
Packing or duct tape

Directions:

1. Blow the balloon up to the size you'd like your piñata to be and tie it off. Tie a piece of string to the neck of the balloon and to a dowel rod, so the balloon will hang while you work on it. Place the dowel rod between two chairs.
2. Cut the newspaper into strips about 1" wide and about 8" long.
3. Make a mixture of half water and half white glue. You may have to stir the mixture occasionally as you work. You'll also want to put this in a bowl that is easy to clean or is disposable.
4. Run the newspaper strips through the glue mixture and remove the extra by running the strip lightly between your fingers. Smooth the strip of newspaper onto the balloon, wiping out any major bumps or wrinkles. Keep applying the strips of paper until the balloon is completely covered. Leave a little bit of balloon showing where the string is tied to the knot. Let the piñata dry overnight.
5. The next day add another similar layer, letting it dry overnight again. Four layers is the maximum to apply, but three is usually sufficient. Make sure each layer is completely dry before adding the next layer. On the last layer, use white paper instead of newspaper. This will make it easier to paint.
6. Once the last layer is dry, pop the balloon and pull it out of the piñata. The piñata is now ready to paint like it is an Easter egg. You can also glue fringed tissue paper in rows like a traditional piñata. See picture on page 38.
7. To hang the piñata, poke four holes around the larger hole at the top. Thread a piece of yarn through each hole and then bring the pieces of yarn together and tie them in a knot. You can attach a longer string to the yarn so that the piñata can hang from a tree limb or an outdoor basketball hoop. Reinforce the piñata where the yarn goes through the holes by applying some packing tape or duct tape on the inside over the yarn and holes. When the piñata is whacked, the yarn may pull through the papier-mâché if not reinforced.
8. Fill with candy and small toys. Blindfold each person before they try to hit and break open the piñata.

Easter Lily

Isaiah 1:18

Though your sins are like scarlet, they shall be as white as snow.

ISAIAH 1:18 (NIV®)

The Easter lily is a beautiful white flower that people use to decorate at church and home during the Easter season. The white flower is a symbol of purity, innocence, and hope. The trumpet shape reminds us to share the good news as we rejoice in the resurrection of Jesus.

The Bible mentions lilies, too. Luke 12:27–30 talks about the lilies of the field. Even though their blooms don't last long, God has made them beautiful, and He takes care of them. When we think about how good God is to a lily, we remember that He loves us even more and will always take care of us when we call to Him for help.

Questions:

1. What are some other things you can think of that are white? What do they have in common?
2. Why does an Easter lily remind us of Jesus?
3. If God takes care of the lilies of the field, what do you think He will do for us?
4. Read Isaiah 1:18. How do our sins change after Jesus forgives us?

Make an Easter lily to help you remember Jesus' resurrection.
Make a whole bouquet and share it with someone you love.

Materials:

White, yellow, and green construction paper
Tape or glue
Pencil, straw, or green chenille pipe cleaner
Scissors

Directions:

1. Trace the lily petal pattern found on page 48 onto a piece of white construction paper. Cut it out and fold the tab along the dotted line as seen on the template. Roll the lily into a cone, overlapping only the tab on the inside of the cone. Tape or glue into place, making sure the edge of the tab is on the edge of the flower. Curl petals tips slightly using a rounded edge of a marker or your fingers.
2. Choose what kind of stem you will use. You can use a green chenille pipe cleaner, a straw, a green pencil, or you can make one out of green construction paper. Just tightly roll a piece of construction paper around a pencil or a straw and tape it together.
3. Trace the stamen pattern onto a piece of yellow construction paper. Cut it out, and fringe one end. Tightly roll the unfringed edge around the stem and tape together. Curl the fringe edge of the stamen if desired.
4. Snip off just the tip of the base of the lily to make a hole large enough for the stem. Push the stem through the hole and pull until you come to the edge of the yellow stamen. Tape the base of the lily to the stem to hold in place.
5. Trace the leaf pattern on this page onto green construction paper. Cut out and wrap the bottom edge around the stem and tape to secure.

Leaf

Craft Stick Puzzle

Philippians 2:5–11

Being found in appearance as a man, he humbled himself by becoming obedient to death—even death on a cross!

PHILIPPIANS 2:8 (NIV®)

The events in Jesus' life that led to His death and resurrection are very important for every Christian to remember. Jesus is God's only Son. God sent Him to earth to show the world His love, teach us the truth about God, and to save each person who believes in Him from an eternity in hell.

Jesus left heaven to become a man. Even though He was the King of kings, He humbled Himself and became like us. Jesus taught us what the Scriptures mean and how to live God's way. Then He took on the sins of the whole world and died on the cross in our place.

Jesus rose to life again and now lives in heaven with God. Jesus said He is going to prepare a place for us, and someday He will come back to take us to heaven. We have a choice while we live on the earth whether or not to follow Jesus. We can choose to believe in Him and obey Him, or not to do so. But the Bible tells us that someday, "every knee should bow…and every tongue acknowledge that Jesus Christ is Lord" (Philippians 2:10–11, NIV®). In the end, everyone will know that Jesus is God's Son and will bow down to honor Him.

Questions:

1. Why was Jesus born?
2. Where is Jesus now?
3. What did Jesus say He was going to do in heaven?
4. Have you asked Jesus to be your Savior? Why or why not?

This puzzle will help you put the events of Jesus' last days on earth in order.

Materials:

7 plain wooden craft sticks
Tape
Scissors or hobby knife
Baggie for storage
Pen or marker
Glue
Paper to draw a picture, or Easter picture from a magazine or coloring book

Directions:

1. Write the first sentence from the list below on a craft stick. Continue until you have written all of the sentences in this order:

    Jesus rides into Jerusalem on a donkey.

    Jesus eats with His disciples.

    Jesus goes to the garden to pray.

    Jesus is arrested.

    Jesus is hung on the cross.

    Jesus is buried in the tomb.

    Jesus rises from the grave!

2. Turn the sticks over, still in order, so the writing is facedown.
3. Leave a very small space between each stick—just enough so you can use the edge of your scissors blade or a knife to cut through later. Then use a long piece of tape to attach two sticks together covering the long edges of the sticks. Continue to attach another stick, until all of the sticks are connected.
4. Cut a piece of paper that will cover all of your sticks and draw a scene from the Easter story in the Bible. Or find a pretty Easter or spring picture in a magazine that you can use. (Ask before you cut it out if the magazine belongs to your parent!)
5. When you are finished with your picture, cover your craft sticks with a small amount of glue. Glue your picture onto the sticks. Let dry.
6. When your project is completely dry, use the blade of your scissors or ask a parent if you can use a knife to cut through the picture to separate the craft sticks.
7. Mix the sticks up and see if you can put the Easter story written on them in order. You will know you have the right answer when you flip the sticks over and the picture is correct.

The Last Supper pg. 14

Figure A

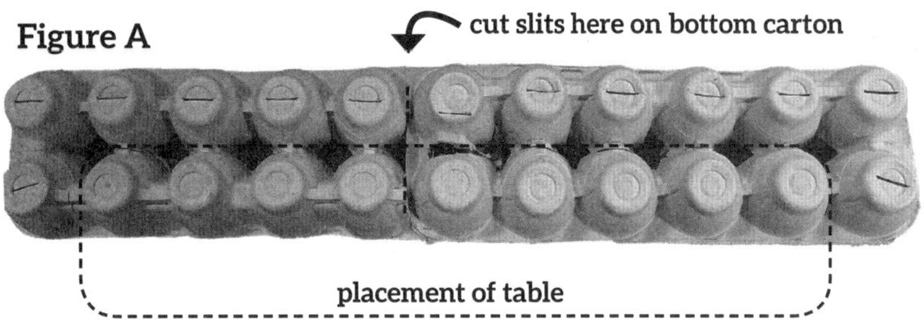

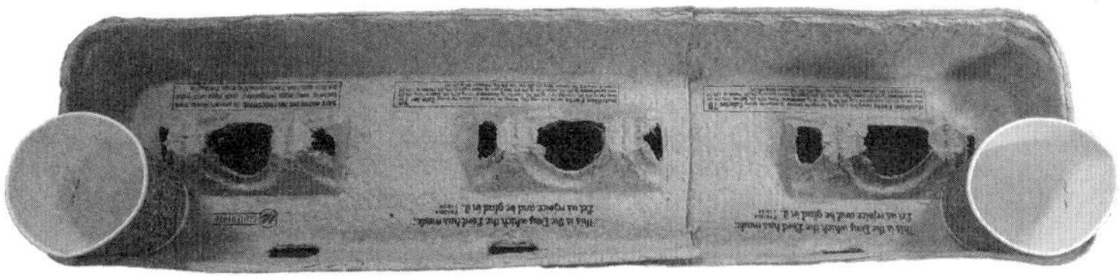

Figure B

Figure C

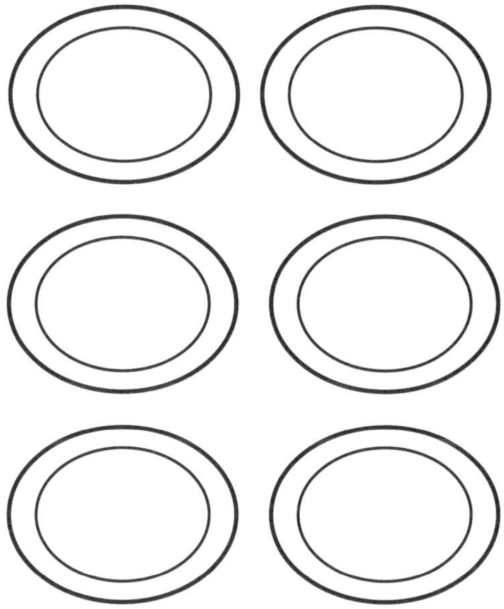

Jesus

John

Andrew

Simon the Zealot

Thaddaeus

Philip

James

Matthew

Thomas

Judas Iscariot

James (son of Alphaeus)

Peter

Bartholomew

Cock-a-doodle Rooster pg. 20

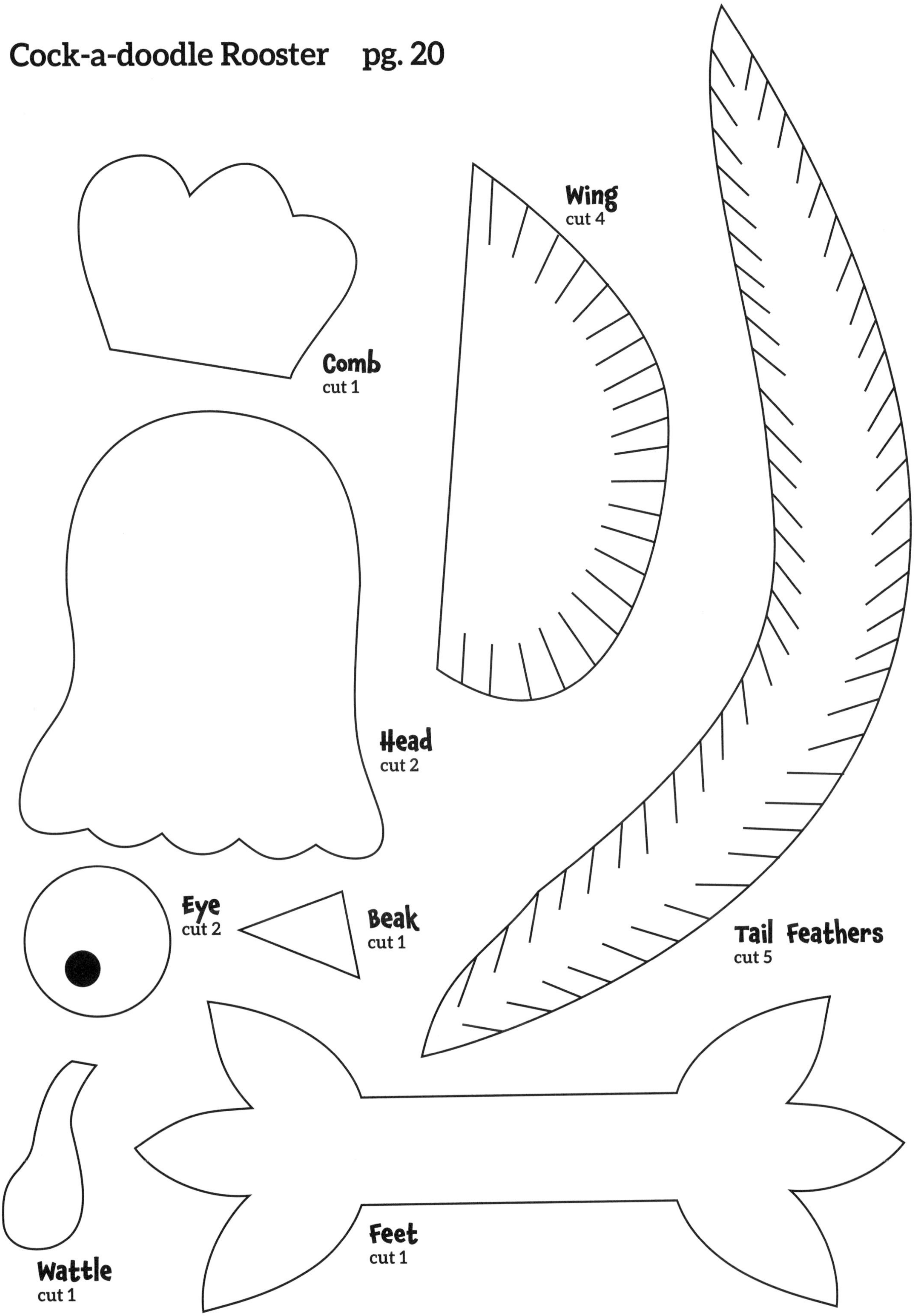

Easter Angel pg. 34

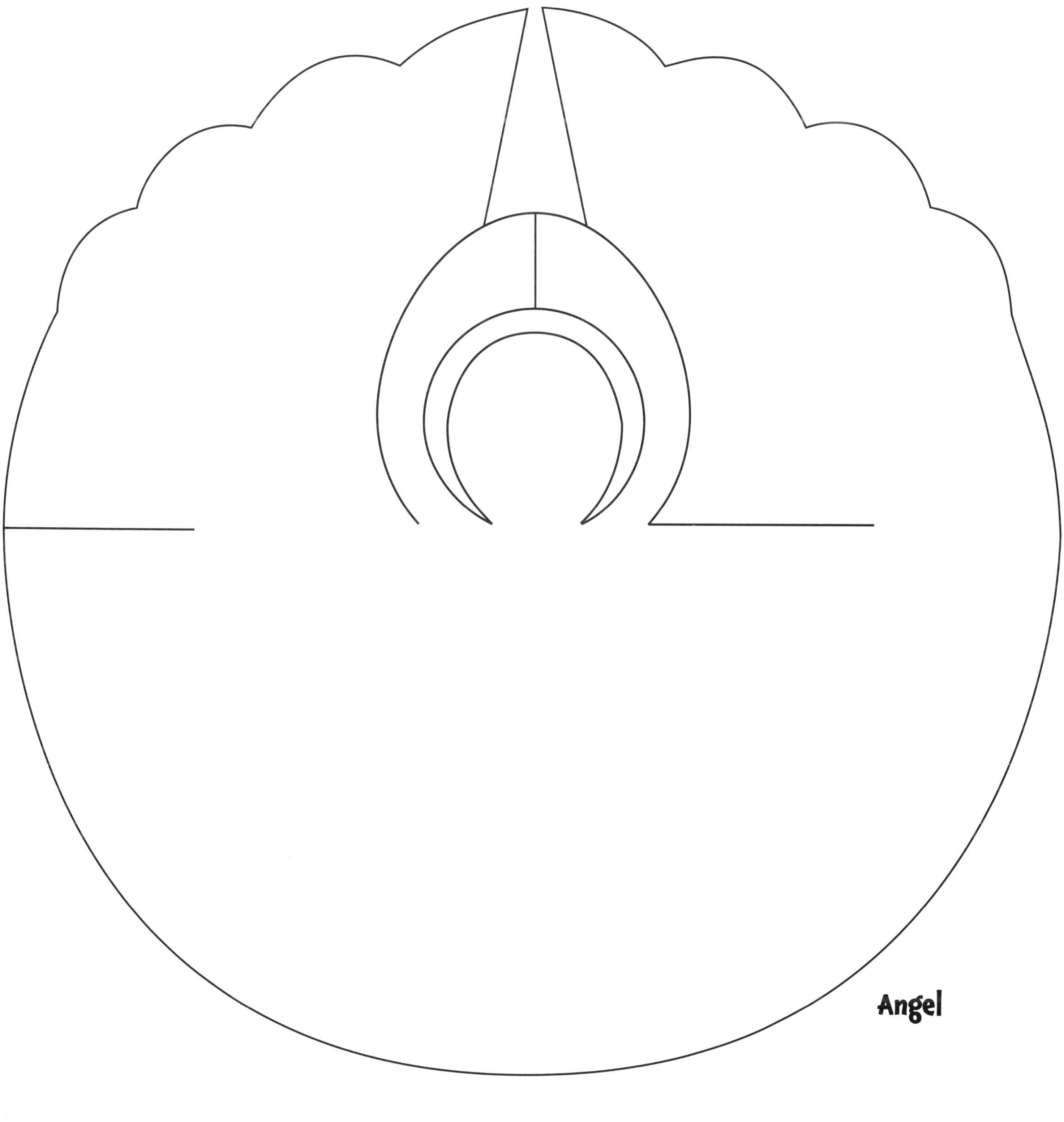

Easter Lily pg. 40

Stamen

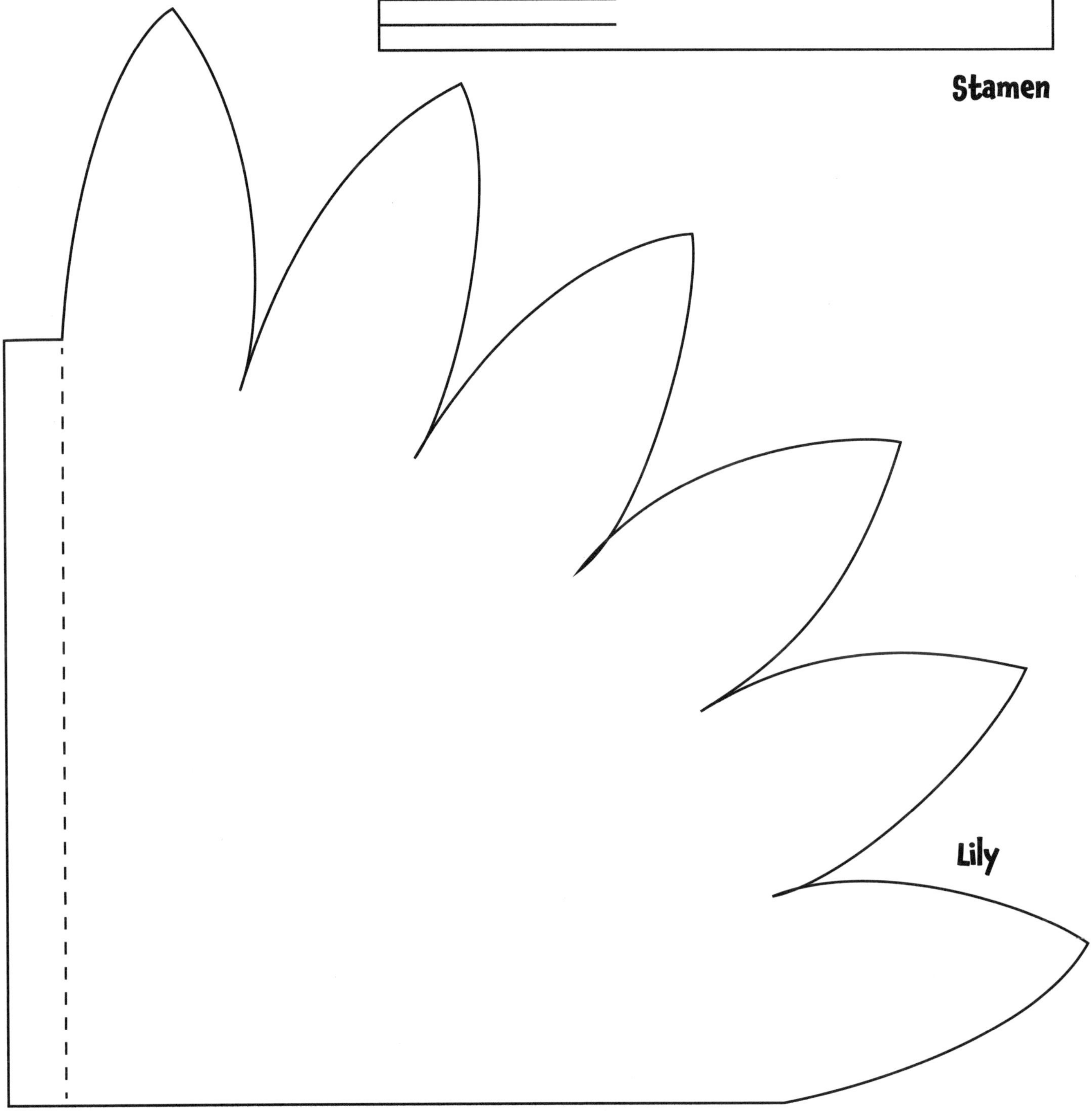